Mr. See-more says "Look Down"

Written by Lucy Kincaid
Illustrated by Eric Kincaid

BRIMAX BOOKS
CAMBRIDGE ENGLAND

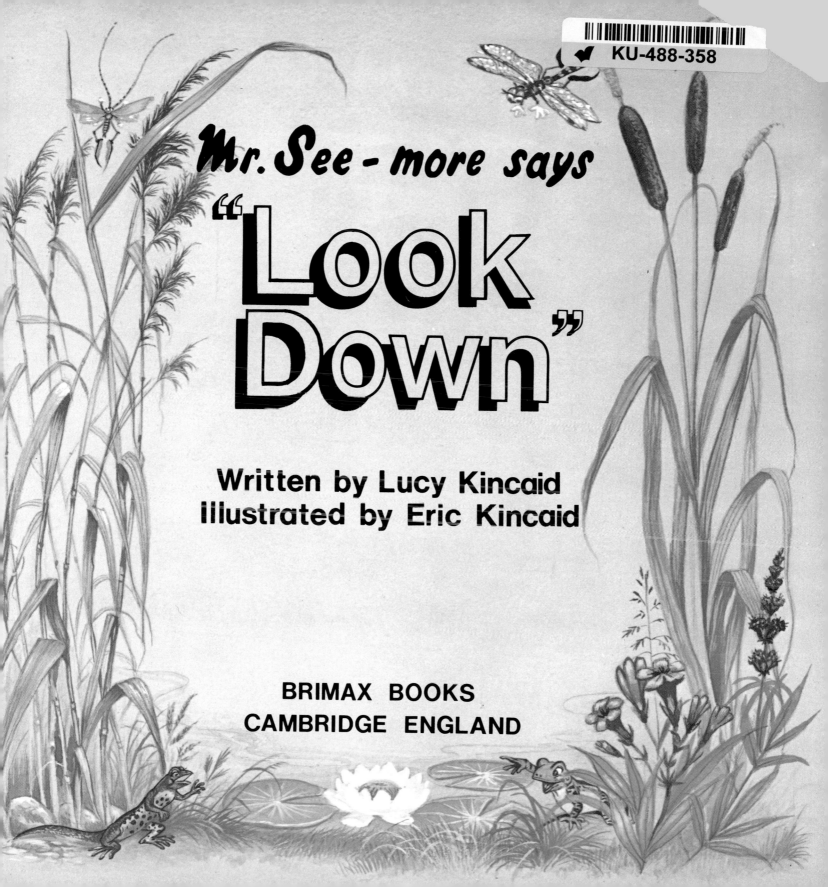

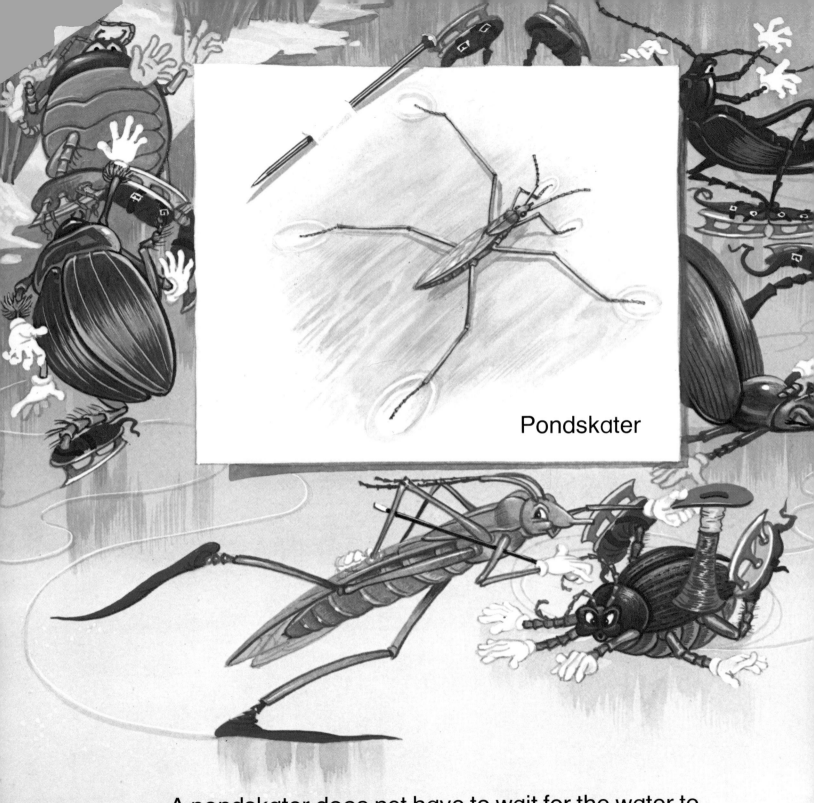

Pondskater

A pondskater does not have to wait for the water to freeze. It can skate all the year round.

Water spider and air bubble

A water spider is a do-it-yourself expert. It makes its own diving bell and fills it with air.

Frog spawn   Tadpoles

A newly hatched tadpole holds onto something very tightly until it gets used to being outside its egg.

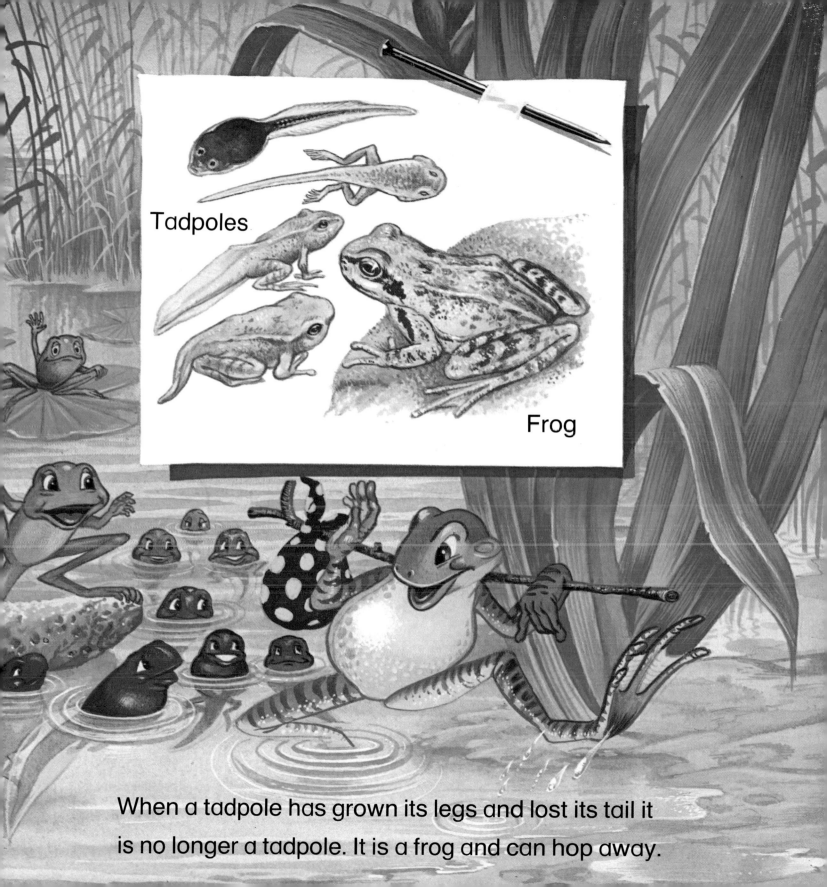

Tadpoles

Frog

When a tadpole has grown its legs and lost its tail it is no longer a tadpole. It is a frog and can hop away.

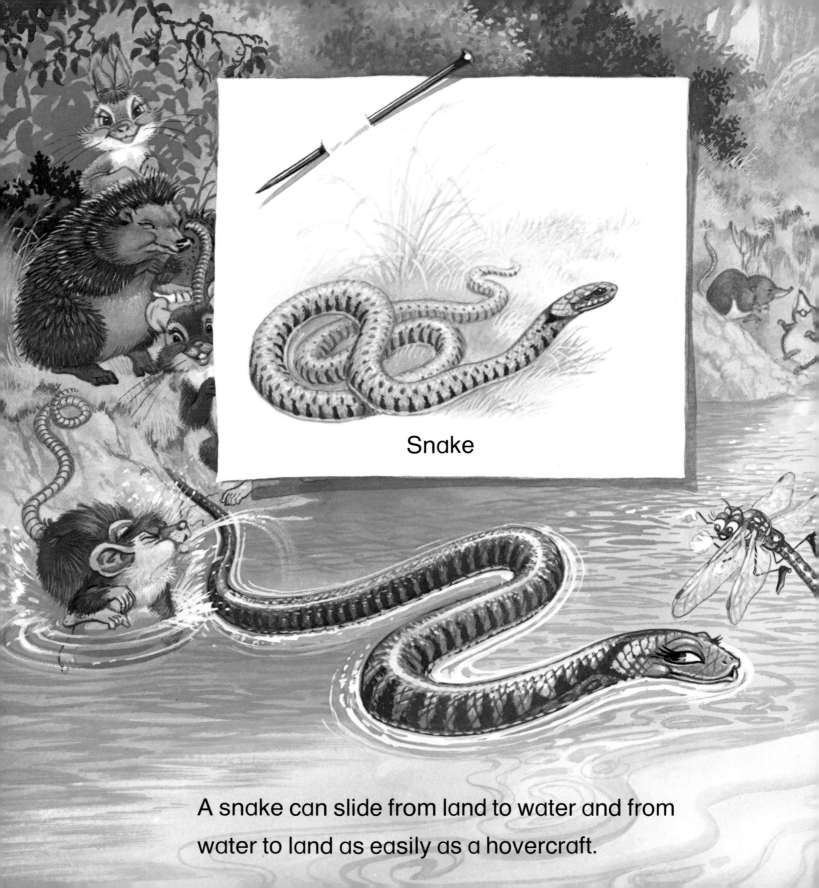

Snake

A snake can slide from land to water and from water to land as easily as a hovercraft.

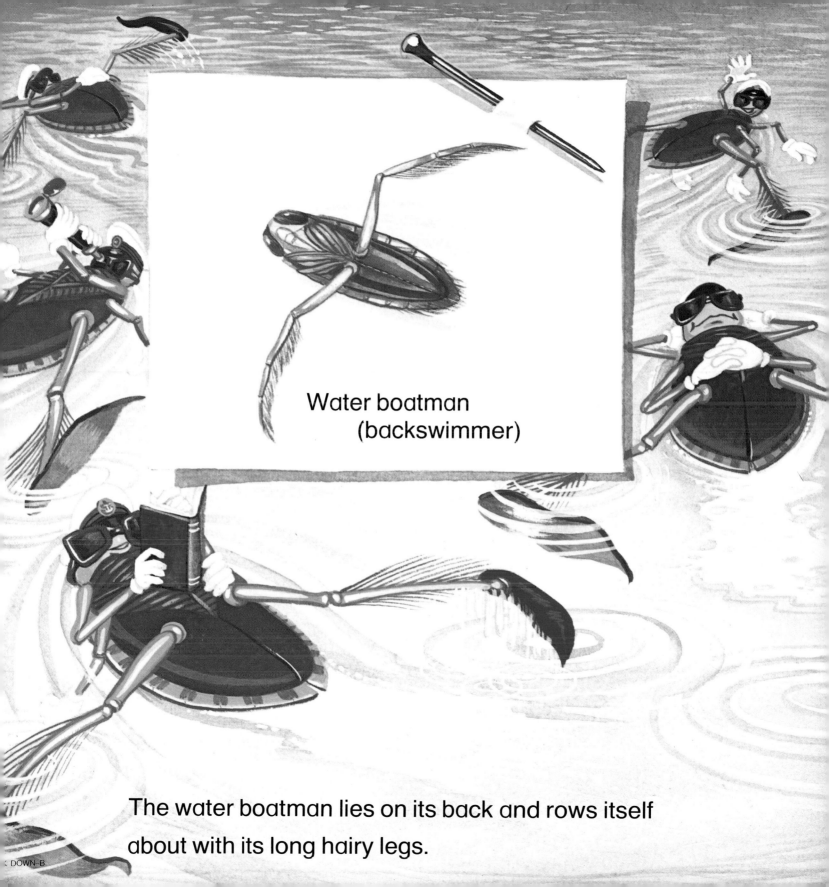

Water boatman
(backswimmer)

The water boatman lies on its back and rows itself about with its long hairy legs.

Water lily

Water lily flowers and leaves are anchored in the mud by long thick stems.

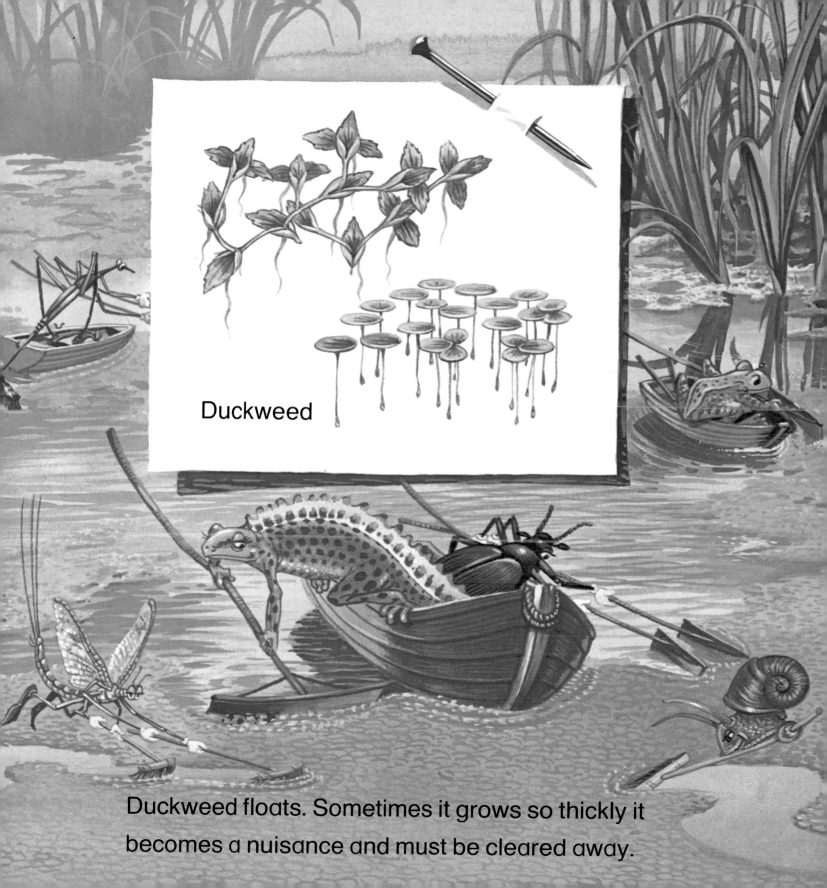

Duckweed

Duckweed floats. Sometimes it grows so thickly it becomes a nuisance and must be cleared away.

Toad

Toad spawn

Toads and frogs are cousins. They can tell their eggs apart because the toad lays hers in long strips.

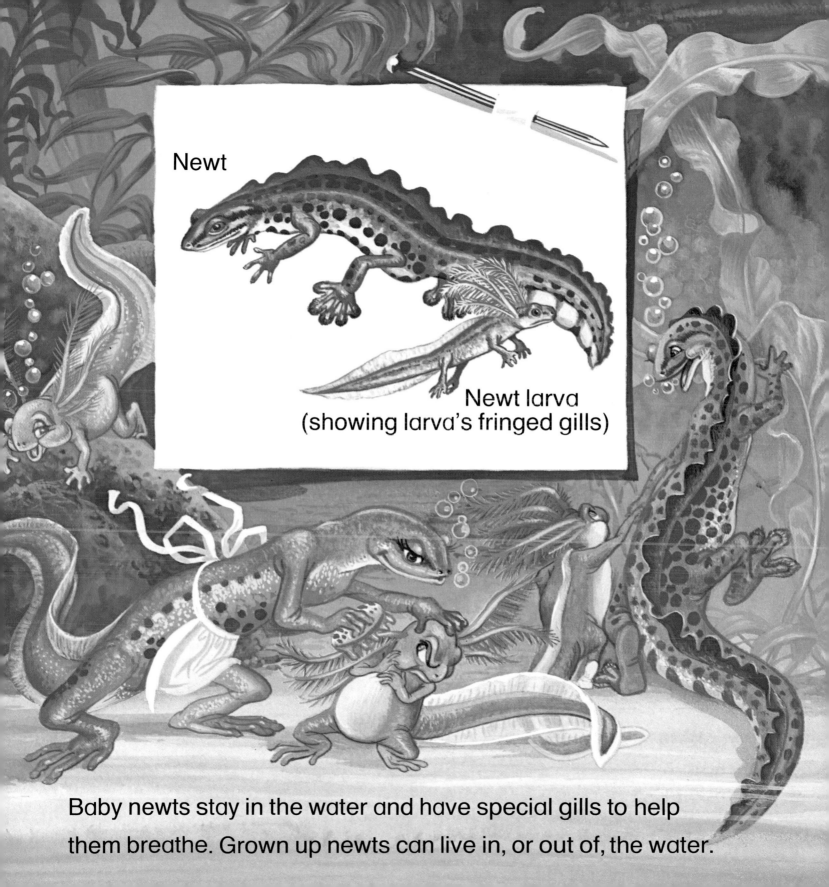

Newt

Newt larva
(showing larva's fringed gills)

Baby newts stay in the water and have special gills to help them breathe. Grown up newts can live in, or out of, the water.

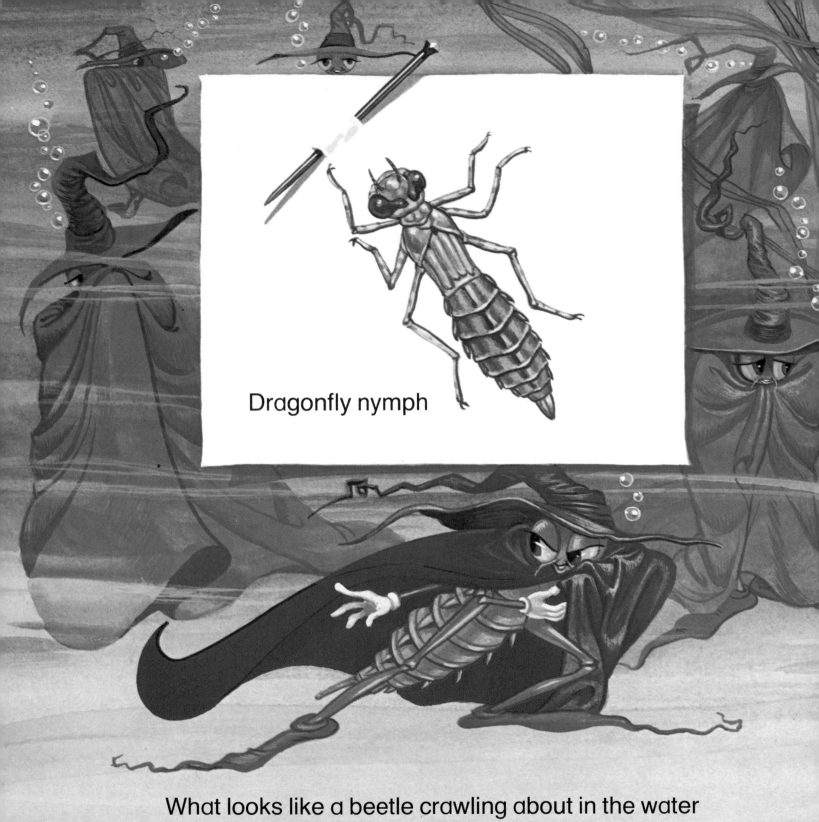

Dragonfly nymph

What looks like a beetle crawling about in the water is sometimes not a beetle. Sometimes it is a nymph.

Dragonfly

Dragonfly emerging
from larva case

One day the nymph will climb up a stem and out of the water. She will throw off her dull brown skin and fly away.

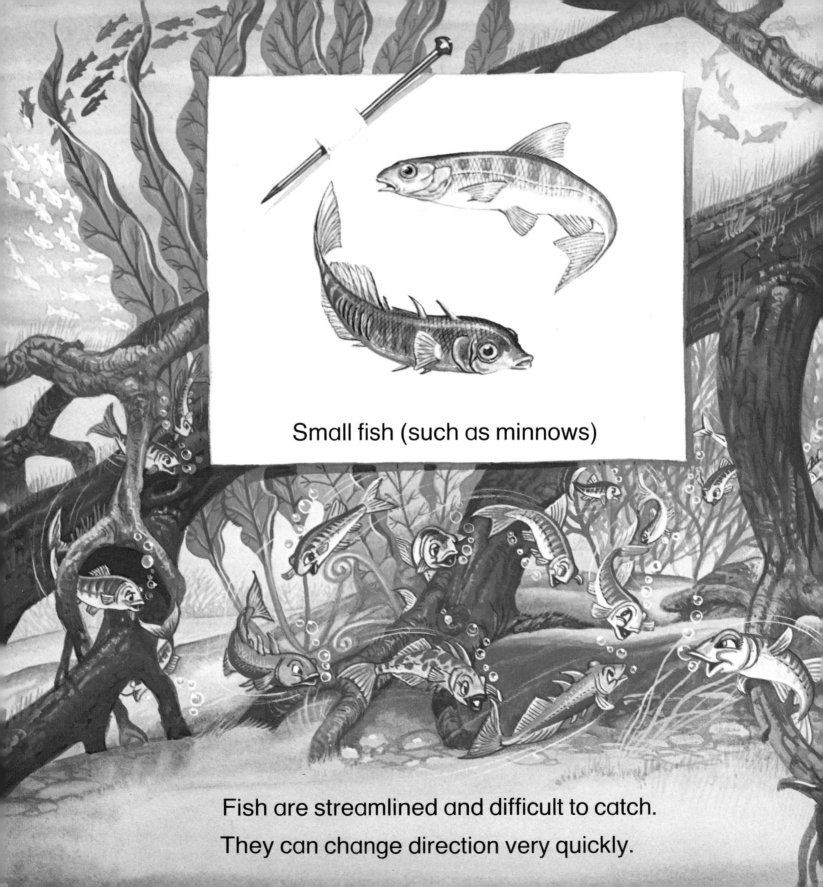

Small fish (such as minnows)

Fish are streamlined and difficult to catch.

They can change direction very quickly.

Whirligig beetle

A whirligig beetle likes to whirl.
It never seems to get giddy.

Caddis fly larvae in their various cases

There is no mistaking a home built by a
caddis fly larva. It is unbelievable.

Flatworms

Not all worms are round like string. Some are flat.
They hardly look like worms at all.

Water snail

A water snail lives in the water because it chooses to, not because it has fallen in.

Water beetle

Which end does a beetle breathe through?

It depends to which family it belongs.

Footprints in the mud

Who made the footprints across the mud?

Who has gone for a swim?